Aurora Michelle
From Grandma & Grandpa Inoennes

# The Beginner's Bible
## Beginner's Bible Treasury

8 books in 1

*"Your faith has healed you."*
—Luke 17:19

ZONDERKIDZ

*The Beginner's Bible Treasury*

Copyright © 2012 by Zondervan
Illustrations © 2012 by Zondervan

Requests for information should be addressed to:

*Zonderkidz, 3900 Sparks Dr. SE, Grand Rapids, Michigan 49546*

ISBN 978-0-310-62157-7

*Jesus Heals the Sick*—ISBN 978-0-310-72518-3 Copyright © 2012 by Zondervan
*Jesus Feeds the Hungry*—ISBN 978-0-310-72519-0 Copyright © 2012 by Zondervan
*Noah and the Big Boat*—ISBN 978-0-310-73673-8 Copyright © 2013 by Zondervan
*Daniel and the Hungry Lions*—ISBN 978-0-310-73674-5 Copyright © 2013 by Zondervan
*David Battles Goliath*—ISBN 978-0-310-74081-0 Copyright © 2013 by Zondervan
*Jesus Shows God's Love*—ISBN 978-0-310-74148-0 Copyright © 2013 by Zondervan
*Joseph in Egypt* ISBN—978-0-310-74149-7 Copyright © 2013 by Zondervan
*A Queen Named Esther*—ISBN 978-0-310-74080-3 Copyright © 2013 by Zondervan

*Written by: Crystal Bowman*
*Editor: Mary Hassinger*
*Cover & Interior Design: Cindy Davis*

*Printed in China*

14 15 16 17 18 19 20 /DSC/ 12 11 10 9 8 7 6 5 4 3 2 1

# Jesus Heals the Sick

One day, Jesus walked into a city where many people wanted to see him.

An army captain hurried to meet him. "Please help me, Lord," he said.
"My servant is home in bed. He is very sick."

"I will go to him and heal him," Jesus said.

"You don't need to come to my house," said the captain.
"Just say the words to make him better. I know he will be healed."

Jesus was amazed at the captain's faith.

He said to the people, "This man has more faith than anyone I have met." Jesus said to the captain, "You may go home now. Your servant is healed because you believed."

When the captain got home, his servant was healed—
just like Jesus had said.

A few days later, Jesus was preaching in a house. The house was so full of people that many had to stand outside.

Four men came to the house to see Jesus. They wanted Jesus to heal their friend who could not walk. They carried their friend on a mat, but they could not get close to Jesus. So they went up to the roof.

The men lowered their friend down through a hole in the roof. He ended up right in front of Jesus! Jesus saw that the men had great faith. He looked at the man who couldn't walk and said, "Your sins are forgiven. Stand up! Take your mat and walk home."

At once, the man stood up. He picked up his mat and walked out the
door. The people were amazed and praised God.

Many people began to hear stories of how Jesus could heal sick people.
Wherever Jesus went people crowded around him.

A man named Jairus came to Jesus and said, "My little girl is dying.
Please come and put your hands on her to make her better."

Jesus went with Jairus to his house. Many people followed them. One person was a woman who had been sick for twelve years. She believed that Jesus could heal her. She tried to get close to Jesus. *If I could touch his clothes, I will be healed*, she thought.

The woman finally got close enough to touch Jesus' clothes. As soon as she touched him, she was healed!

"Who touched me?" Jesus asked.

The woman was afraid, but she went to Jesus and bowed at his feet.

"I touched your clothes, so you could heal me," she said.

"Go in peace," said Jesus. "You are well because you believed."

When Jesus came to Jairus' house, the people told Jairus that his daughter had died. "It's too late!" they said.

Jesus said to Jairus, "Don't be afraid. Just believe." Then Jesus said to the people, "Why are you crying? She is only sleeping."

Jesus told the people to leave the house. He went to see the girl.
Jairus and his wife, and three of Jesus' helpers, went with him.
Jesus took the girl's hand and said, "Little girl, get up."

Right away the girl got up and walked around the room! Jairus and his wife were very happy that Jesus had healed their daughter!

Later, as Jesus was walking along, he met a man who was blind. The man sat on the ground and begged for money and food. Jesus' disciples asked him, "Was this man born blind because he sinned, or because his parents sinned?"

"He is not blind because of sin," Jesus said. "He was born blind so that God's power can be shown in his life." Then Jesus spit on the ground and made some mud. He put the mud on the blind man's eyes. "Go and wash in the Pool of Siloam," Jesus said.

The blind man did what Jesus told him to do. He washed off the mud, and suddenly he could see!

The people were surprised! "How can you see?" they asked.

The man told everyone how Jesus had healed him, and they were all amazed.

As Jesus was on his way to Jerusalem, he met ten men who were lepers. They had bad sores all over their bodies. They shouted to Jesus, "Please help us, Jesus! Make us well!"

Jesus said to them, "Go to the priests and show yourselves to them."
As the men were walking to find the priests, their sores began to get better!
Soon the sores were all gone! The men were healed—all ten of them!

One man hurried back to Jesus. The other men walked away.

The man bowed down before Jesus. "Thank you, Lord!" he said. Jesus said to him, "Go. Your faith has made you well."

Jesus healed sick people because he was the Son of God. Many people who saw or heard of his miracles began to believe in Jesus.

*"They don't need to go away.*
*You give them something to eat."*
—Matthew 14:16

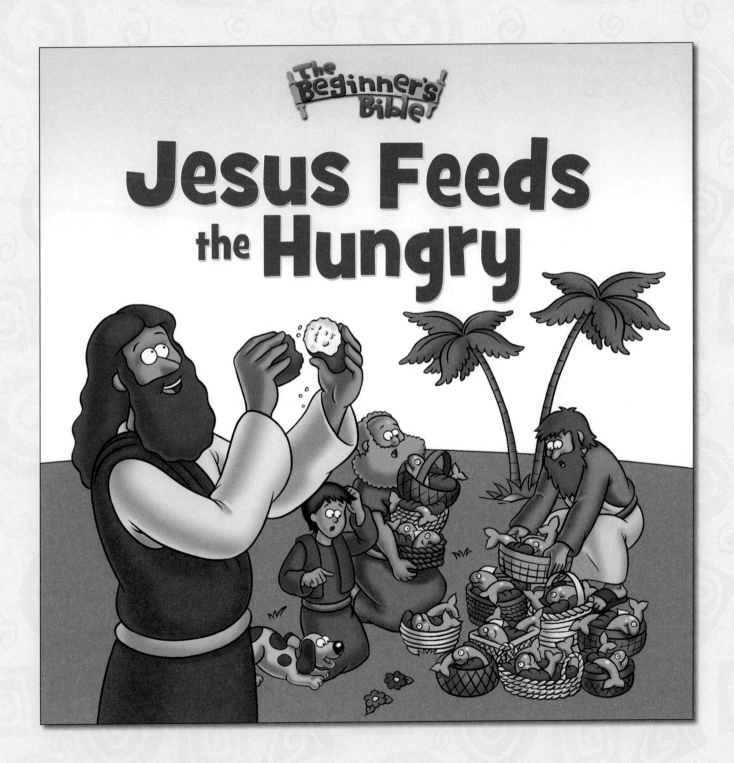

Many people followed Jesus wherever he went. Some of the people wanted Jesus to heal them. Some wanted to ask him questions. Others just wanted to listen to his stories. Jesus loved the people very much. But sometimes Jesus was tired, and he wanted to be alone in a quiet place, where he could rest.

One day, Jesus got into a boat with Philip, Andrew, John, and his other disciples. They went across the lake so they could get away from the crowd for a while and rest. But they couldn't get away. The people ran along the shore to the place where Jesus was going. They ran so fast they got there before Jesus did.

When the boat reached the shore, the people were waiting for Jesus.
Jesus climbed out of the boat and walked toward the people.

He looked at the big crowd and felt sorry for them. He knew they had come especially to see him, so he did not want to send them away. Jesus spent time with the people. He placed his hands on the sick people and healed them.

Jesus talked to the people and taught them many things. He told them that God loved them. He told them to be kind to others. He told them to obey God and to do what was right. The people stayed and listened to Jesus for a long, long time.

Soon the sun was going down, and it was getting late in the day.

The disciples were worried. They said to Jesus, "It's already late, and there is nothing to eat around here. Send the people to the nearby towns so they can find food to eat and places to sleep."

But Jesus said to Philip, "Don't send them away. We need to feed them. Where can we buy bread so we will have enough food to feed all these people?" Jesus said this to see what Philip would say. He already knew what he was going to do.

Philip shook his head and said, "We cannot feed this many people! We would have to work many months in order to earn enough money to buy food for them."

"How much food do we have right now?" asked Jesus.
"Go and find out."

Andrew found a boy who had some food. He brought the boy to Jesus.

"Here is a boy who will share his food with us," said Andrew.
"But he only has five loaves of barley bread and two small fish.
That is not enough to feed this big, hungry crowd."

Jesus said to his disciples, "Tell everyone to sit down on the grass. Have them sit in groups of about fifty people."

So that is what they did. All of the men, women, and children sat down on the grass in groups. They waited to see what Jesus would do.

Jesus took a loaf of bread in his hands and looked up toward heaven. He thanked God for the bread and asked God to bless it. He broke the loaves of bread into pieces and gave the pieces to his disciples to give to the people.

Then Jesus took the fish in his hands and thanked God for the fish. He asked God to bless the fish, and he broke them into pieces—just like he did with the bread. Jesus gave the pieces of fish to his disciples so they could feed the people.

The disciples gave the bread and fish to the people. And to the disciples' surprise they never ran out of food! They had enough bread and fish to feed everyone. Over five thousand people ate until their stomachs were full. There was even food left over!

Jesus said to his disciples, "Pick up the pieces of fish and bread that are left over. Do not waste any of the food." So the disciples picked up all the pieces of bread and fish that had not been eaten, and they put the food into baskets. There was enough food left over to fill twelve large baskets!

When the people saw this miracle that Jesus had done, they knew he was not an ordinary man.

"He must be the Prophet we have been waiting for!" they said.

Jesus knew it was time for him to leave the people for a while.
So he went up into the hills where he could rest, be alone, and pray.

*Noah did everything exactly as God commanded him.*
—Genesis 6:22

When God made the world, everything was perfect. The grass was green. The sky was blue. The trees and flowers were pretty. And the birds sang happy songs.

God made a man and a woman to live in this perfect world. But soon the man and woman disobeyed God's one rule. God still loved them, but his world was not perfect anymore.

After a while, many more people lived in the world. They did not
always love God or obey him. They were mean to each other and did
some very bad things.

God was sad that the people were so bad. He was sorry that he had made people to live in his beautiful world.

But there was one man who loved God. His name was Noah. Noah's family loved God too. God was happy that Noah and his family loved him.

One day, God said to Noah, "The people do not obey me. They do bad things every day. I do not want them to live in my world anymore. I am going to send a flood to wash everything away." But God wanted Noah to be safe. So God told Noah to build a big boat.

"You must build an ark from wood," God said. "It needs to be very big and tall. Make rooms in the ark and cover it with tar. It will be for you and your family. It will also be for the animals. Two of every kind will come to you."

Noah did not know how to build an ark. But God told him just what to do. Noah listened to God and did everything God told him to do.

Noah worked very hard every day. It took many years for Noah to
build the ark. But Noah never gave up. He worked, and he worked, and
he worked.

Finally the ark was finished. Now it was time to put the animals inside. The animals came to Noah two-by-two, just like God said they would.

Noah led the animals into the ark. Birds and bears. Rabbits and dogs. Turtles and donkeys. Cats and spiders. Every kind of animal went into the ark.

Noah had to bring a lot of food into the ark for his family and for all the animals.

Some of the animals were much harder to get into the ark! But Noah obeyed God and did everything God told him to do.

Noah finally got all the food and animals into the ark. Then it was time for Noah and his family to go into the ark too. When everyone was safe inside, God closed the door.

Big raindrops began to fall from the sky. It rained and rained and rained. It rained for forty days and forty nights. Soon the whole earth was covered with water. Even the tallest mountains were covered with water.

Noah and his family were safe and dry inside the ark. The animals were safe too. And they all had enough food to eat. God kept them safe, just like he had promised.

The rain finally stopped. But Noah and his family and all the animals had to stay inside the ark for many more days.

God sent a wind to blow across the water to make the flood go away.
Noah opened a window in the ark and sent out a dove. He was hoping the
dove could find some dry land. But soon the dove came back to the ark.
The water was still too high.

One week later, Noah sent the dove out again. This time the dove came back with a leaf in its mouth. Noah knew that the flood was almost gone. He sent the dove out one more time. This time the dove did not come back. Noah knew they would soon be able to come out of the ark.

*Bump!* "What was that?" asked Noah. He looked over the side of the ark. Noah saw that the water was drying up. "It's time for you and your family to leave the ark," God told Noah. "Let all the animals out too!"

Noah and his family and all the animals came out of the ark. Noah thanked God for keeping them safe. God said to Noah, "I promise I will never send another flood to cover the earth." Then God put a beautiful rainbow in the sky.

*May God be praised for ever and ever!*
—Daniel 2:20

Daniel was a man who loved God. King Darius liked Daniel because he was such a hard worker. So King Darius chose Daniel to be one of his main helpers. The king wanted to put Daniel in charge of *everything*.

The king had other helpers too. They did not love God like Daniel did. And they did not want the king to put Daniel in charge of everything. They wanted to find a way to get rid of Daniel.

The men tried to find something wrong with Daniel. But Daniel
always did what was right. They could not find anything wrong with him.

The men who did not like Daniel finally thought of a plan to get rid of him. They said to the king, "You are such a great king! You are so great and wise that people should pray to you! You should make a new law that says everyone must pray only to you for the next thirty days. If they do not obey the law, they must be put into the lions' den."

King Darius thought about this idea for a while. Since he was the king, he could make any law he wanted to. But he did not know this idea was a trick to hurt his friend Daniel.

The men who didn't like Daniel waited to see what the king would do.
They hoped the king would agree to their idea.

King Darius did like the idea of people praying to him. "Okay," he said to the men. "I will make it a law." The king signed the law and put his seal on it. Now no one could change the law—not even the king.

For the next thirty days, the people could only pray to King Darius. If they did not obey the law, they would be put into the lions' den.

Daniel always prayed to God, three times every day. When Daniel heard about the king's new law, he didn't stop praying to God. Daniel went home and prayed, just like he had done the day before.

The men who wanted to hurt Daniel sneaked around outside his
house. They looked in the window and saw Daniel praying to God.
Their mean trick had worked. Now they could finally get rid of Daniel.

The men quickly ran to find King Darius. They couldn't wait to tell him about Daniel. "Oh, King!" said the men. "Didn't you make a law that says the people may only pray to you for the next thirty days?" "Yes, I did," King Darius said. "And isn't it true that whoever prays to anyone but you must be thrown into the lions' den?" the men asked. "Yes, that is true," the king said.

"Well," said the men, "we saw Daniel praying to his God! So now he must be put into the lions' den!"

King Darius was very sad, but he had to follow the law he had made.
He sent guards to Daniel's house.

The guards brought Daniel to the lions' den. Daniel could hear the lions roar.

King Darius was sorry he had made that law. He did not want Daniel to get hurt. But there was nothing he could do.

The king said to Daniel, "I hope your God will keep you safe."

King Darius went back to his house. He did not feel like eating. He was very worried about Daniel. He did not sleep all night.

But Daniel was not worried. He prayed to God, and God sent an angel to keep him safe. The lions did not bite Daniel. They didn't even scratch him. The lions did not hurt Daniel at all.

The next morning King Darius ran to the lions' den. He ran as fast as he could go! He wanted to see if Daniel was all right.

When King Darius reached the lions' den, he called out to Daniel,
"Are you okay, Daniel? Did your God save you from the lions?" "Yes, I
am okay!" said Daniel. "God sent an angel to keep me safe." King Darius
was very happy. "Get Daniel out of the den!" he said.

King Darius wanted everyone to know about Daniel's God. He told all of the people, "Daniel's God saved him from the lions. He is great and mighty! He is the one we must pray to. Daniel's God is the only true God!"

*"The battle belongs to the Lord."*
—1 Samuel 47b

God's people, the Israelites, had a strong army. They protected their families and friends. They made sure the land God gave them was safe too.

But there were people named the Philistines who did not like the Israelites. They had a big and strong army too. The Philistine army wanted to fight against the Israelites.

And they had a very big and strong soldier named Goliath.

"Send your best soldier to fight me," Goliath said. "If he wins the fight the Philistines will be your slaves. If I win, the Israelites will be slaves for the Philistines."

King Saul heard what the giant had to say. His Israelite army was scared.

"He is too big and strong."

"It is too dangerous to fight a man like Goliath."

They ran and hid from the Philistine giant. Goliath stood in front of the army many times, trying to get someone to fight. But no one would even try.

David was a young shepherd. He took care of his father's sheep.

He knew that God would always be by his side to help. So David was happy.

One day young David visited the Israelite army's camp. His brothers were soldiers in the army.

David said, "I am here to bring you food and supplies from our father."

David spent some time with his brothers at the army's camp. While he was still there he heard Goliath make his daily threat. "Come on, Israelites! Don't you have anyone in your army brave enough to fight with me?" Goliath shouted.

David said to his brothers, "I will fight this giant."

But he was young and small and the soldiers laughed. Even David's brothers thought it was not a good idea.

King Saul heard what David said. He asked to see this shepherd boy
who wanted to fight the nine-foot tall giant! When he saw David, Saul said,
"There is no way you could beat Goliath."

But David thought the king was wrong.

David said, "God will be with me. He protects me from other dangers when I am tending my father's sheep. He will always be at my side."

So Saul said, "Go, and may the Lord be with you as you battle."

He gave David the royal armor and helmet to wear. But it was too heavy for David.

David took the armor off and went out to fight Goliath.
He was not scared at all. He knew that God would be like
armor and protect him from the giant.

Before he faced the giant, David went to a nearby stream. He chose five smooth stones and put them in his bag. With his slingshot in his other hand, he went to battle.

David saw Goliath and Goliath saw David. The giant laughed because David was so young and small. He said, "You are so small. I will beat you for sure!"

But David did not care.

David said, "I come before you in the name of the
Lord who rules over all."

David put a stone in his sling and swung it around his head. He let the stone fly and WHAP!

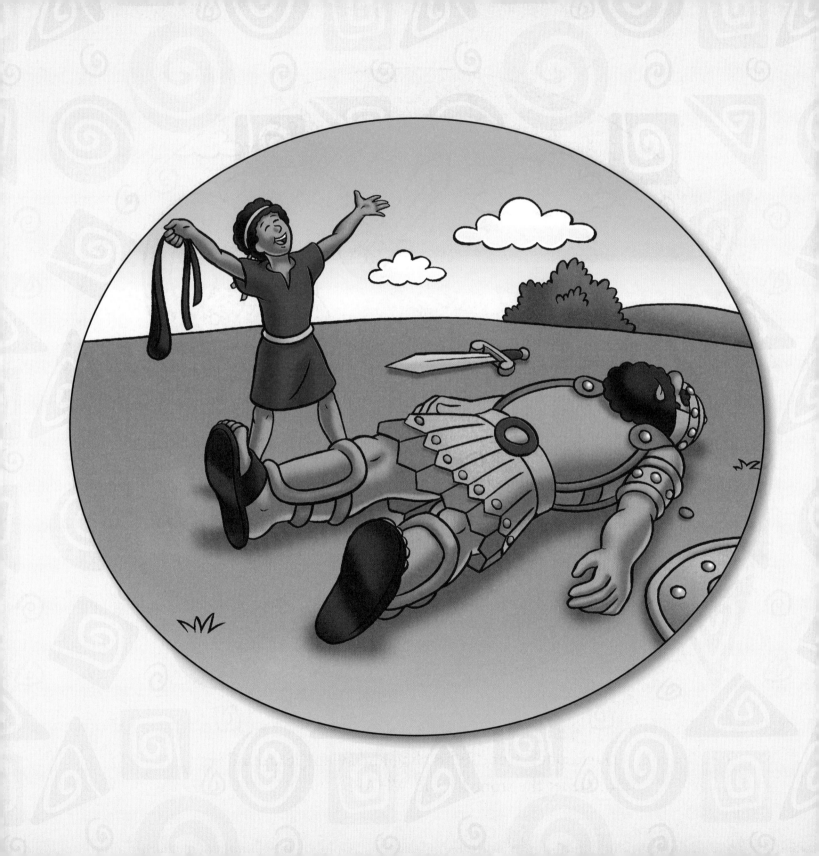

The stone hit Goliath's forehead. The Philistine soldier fell. God had given David strength and courage to face the giant. And he won the fight!

The other Philistine soldiers saw what had happened to their hero. Goliath was dead! They became scared and ran away.

The men in King Saul's army were filled with joy!
Young David was a hero. They shouted their praise and
thanks to God.

"God is great!" the soldiers yelled.
"Thank you, God!" said David.

A voice from heaven said, "This is my Son, whom I love; with him I am well pleased."
—Matthew 3:17

When Jesus was born, it was a special day.
God gave the world a great and wonderful gift.
Jesus was finally here and he was going to save us!

Even angels came to earth and sang praises, "Glory to God in the highest! Peace to everyone on earth."

Jesus grew up, just like everyone else. He lived with his mother Mary and his father Joseph. They taught him to be a good boy.

And Jesus grew up to be a good and caring man.

One day, Jesus went to see his cousin John.
John lived in the wilderness and preached about Jesus
to many people.

John also baptized people.
He said, "Get ready! The Lord is on his way!"

When he saw John, Jesus asked, "Will you please baptize me?"
John was surprised. He thought Jesus should baptize him.
But Jesus said, "John, my Father says you should do this."
And so John baptized Jesus.

Now Jesus was finally ready. God wanted Jesus to teach the world about love.

And so Jesus started work right away. "I will need some help," he thought.

Jesus found twelve good men to help him. Some of the men were fishermen. They left their boats and became teachers with Jesus.

Jesus said to his new friends, "Come with me. Help me teach about my Father's love."

And the men said, "We are happy to be your disciples."

Jesus told his friends about God.
He said, "Love your enemies, do good to those who hate you."

When they were all ready, Jesus and his friends walked and walked to many cities. They talked and talked to many people.

Jesus' message was always about love.
He said, "Love each other as you love yourself."

The disciples had the same message of love.
They said, "Listen to Jesus. He is here because God loves you."

People believed in Jesus' message of love. They came to him for help.

They listened to his words as he taught them to pray.
Jesus said, "Pray like this ... 'Our Father in heaven, hallowed
be your name ...'"

Even when Jesus and his disciples were tired, the people wanted to
listen more to Jesus.

So Jesus and his disciples did not stop talking about God's love.

And everyone, the young and the old that heard Jesus and the disciples speak, knew that God loved them very much.

*But don't be upset. And don't be angry with yourselves because you sold me here. God sent me ahead of you to save many lives.*
—Genesis 45:5

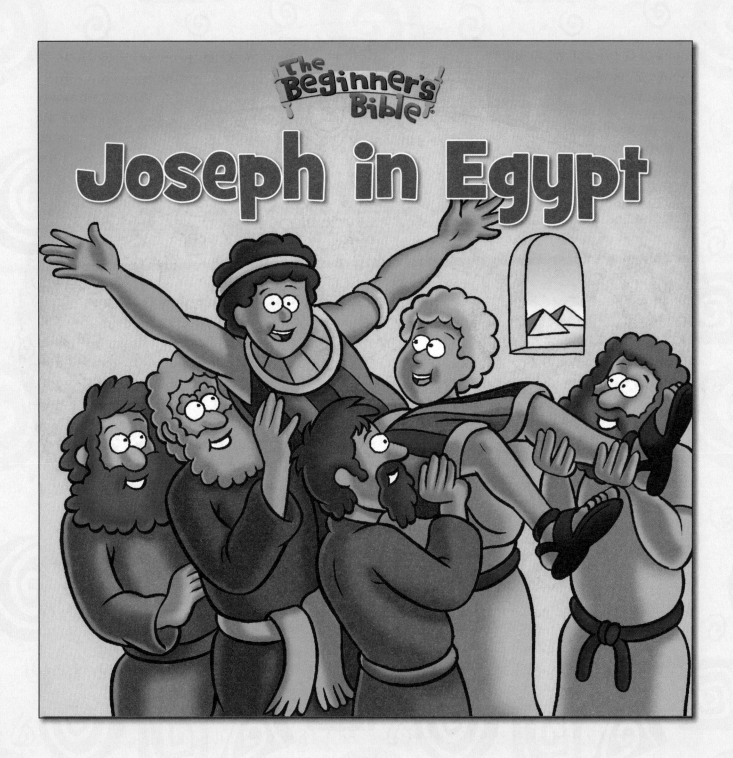

Jacob was a good man. He loved God and God loved him.
God blessed Jacob with twelve sons. They were all good men.

Jacob loved all of his sons. But his favorite son was Joseph.

To show Joseph that he loved him the most Jacob gave him
a very colorful robe. This made Joseph's brothers angry.

They were even angrier when Joseph told them about a dream he had. He said the dream meant the whole family would someday bow to him!

"We must do something about this," one brother said.
"Yes! We need to get rid of Joseph," said another.
And so the brothers threw Joseph into a dry well.

They planned on leaving Joseph in the well. But Joseph's brother Judah
saw some traders coming.

He said, "Do not hurt our brother. Let's sell him to those traders."

So Joseph was taken far away.

The traders took Joseph to a place called Egypt. He worked hard for his boss. But one day Joseph was sent to jail.
He stayed there a long time, but God was always with him.

Joseph liked helping people. He made friends when he was in jail. He even helped one of his new friends understand a dream he had one night.

That new friend left the jail, but he remembered how Joseph had helped him.
So one day, when Pharaoh had a dream, the man told Pharaoh about Joseph.
The man said, "I know Joseph can help you understand your dream too."

Pharaoh let Joseph out of jail. Joseph told Pharaoh his dream was about Egypt. Joseph said, "There will be seven years with enough food. Then there will be seven years with very little food."

Pharaoh listened to Joseph.

He said, "You are wise, Joseph. Help us get ready for this. Please work for me."

Joseph worked hard for Pharaoh. He helped the people save food.
And when the food did stop growing, Egypt was ready!
Joseph helped save many people.

Other countries had a hard time growing food too. Even Joseph's family back home did not have enough to eat.

So Jacob sent his sons to Egypt. He hoped they would find food in the big city.

The brothers went to see the man in charge. They did not know the man in charge was Joseph, their brother. But Joseph knew his brothers. He sold them food and sent them home.

Sometime later, the brothers returned to Egypt. They needed more food. The brothers bowed to Joseph just like in his dream.

Finally Joseph said, "I am your brother!" Now the brothers were afraid. "How could you be Joseph? You have been gone many years!" the brothers said.

"Do not be scared," said Joseph. "I forgive you. God had a job for me here in Egypt. It was part of God's plan to help his people," he explained.

"Now go back home. Get our father, Jacob, and bring him back to Egypt," Joseph told his brothers.

"Thank you, brother!" they all cheered. "God is good!"

*"It's possible that you became*
*queen for a time just like this."*
—Esther 4:14

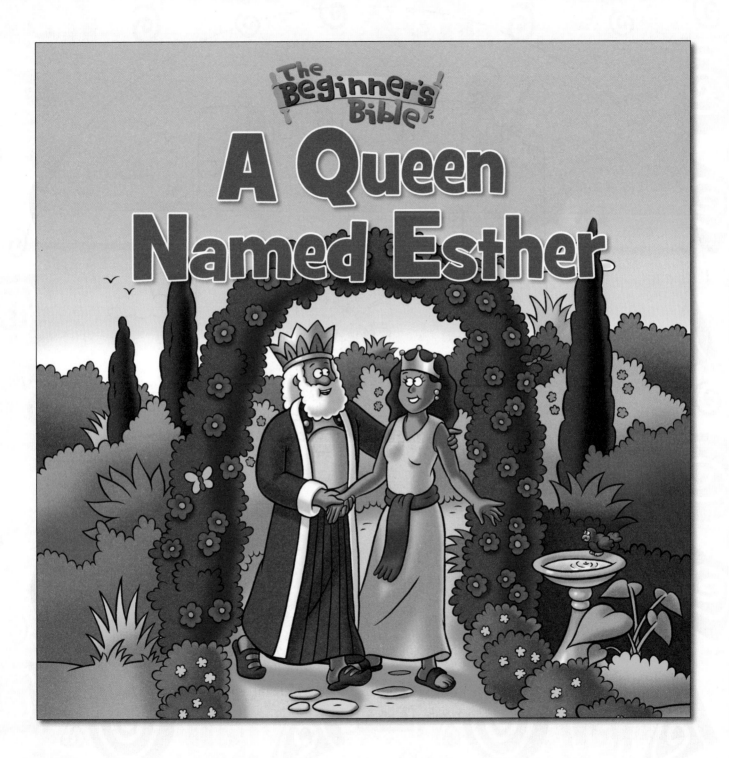

Long, long ago, in a kingdom named Persia, there was a king
that needed a new queen.

His helpers said, "King Xerxes, let us help you find
the perfect girl to be your queen."
King Xerxes thought about it. "Yes, find me the perfect queen."

The king's helpers found a girl named Esther. She was Jewish. Esther lived with her cousin, Mordecai. The men wanted Esther to meet the king.

Mordecai said to her, "Go and meet the king. It is a good idea."

So Esther met the king.
King Xerxes said, "You will be a very good queen."
And soon, she became Queen Esther!

Now, the king had many people helping him. Haman was the king's main helper. He was not a nice man. He hated Jewish people. Haman wanted them to go away. So he talked King Xerxes into making a new law. This law put all the Jewish people in danger.

Mordecai heard about the new law. He had to tell Esther!
Maybe she could help the Jews since she was now the queen.

"Esther!" Mordecai said. "God made you queen for a good reason. You must help save God's people from Haman's evil plan. Please talk to the king. Only he can save us."

Esther knew she had to help. It would not be easy. But she thought of a plan.

"Please help me be strong and brave, God," Esther prayed. "I need to go talk with the king."

"King Xerxes, may I ask you something?" Esther said.

"Yes," said the king. "Please ask me for anything. I will try to give it to you."

Esther said, "I am making a nice dinner. I would like you and your helper Haman to join me."

The king said yes.

So King Xerxes and Haman went to eat dinner with Queen Esther. They were very happy. The food was delicious.

The king asked Esther, "Now, Esther, what can I do for you?"

Esther said, "Haman tricked you! You signed a law. It says to get rid of all the Jews. King Xerxes, I am a Jew too!"

Haman could not believe his ears. Esther knew about his plan.
Now he would not get his way. The Jews would be safe.

King Xerxes was very angry. He could not believe his helper, Haman,
would do this evil thing. He did not like being tricked!

The king called his guards.
He said, "Get Haman. Arrest him now."
The guards took Haman away. He would not be able to hurt the Jews ever again.

Now the king needed a new helper. He knew Queen Esther's cousin, Mordecai, was a good man. He asked Mordecai to be his helper now. Mordecai said, "Yes!"

The king was happy. He knew Esther and Mordecai were good people to have as helpers in his kingdom.

Esther and Mordecai were happy. They were glad they could help the king and God's people.

God's people were very happy too. Esther was a hero. She had saved the Jews from Haman's plan. They were all safe. "Hooray for Queen Esther!" they cheered.

God used Esther to save his people. Thank you, God!